GARDENS

HISTORY
GARDENING
PLANT SCIENCE

Amanda Bennett

This book belongs to

_____

Gardens:
History, Gardening, Plant Science

ISBN 1-888306-01-7

Copyright © 1996 by Amanda Bennett

Published by:
Homeschool Press
229 S. Bridge St.
P.O. Box 254
Elkton, MD 21922-0254

Send requests for information to the above address.

Cover design by Mark Dinsmore.

Printed in the United States of America.

To Uncle Dwight and Aunt Mary,

for showing me just how much a garden

can mean to a family and a community.

Many thanks for a lifetime of memories!

How To Use This Guide

Welcome to the world of unit studies! They present a wonderful method of learning for all ages and it is a great pleasure to share this unit study with you. This guide has been developed and written to provide a basic framework for the study, along with plenty of ideas and resources to help round out the learning adventure. All the research is done. These are READY to go!

TO BEGIN: The <u>Outline</u> is the study "skeleton", providing an overall view of the subject and important subtopics. It can be your starting point— read through it and familiarize yourself with the content. It is great for charting your course over the next few weeks (or developing lesson plans). Please understand that you do not necessarily have to proceed through the outline in order. I personally focus on the areas that our children are interested in first—giving them "ownership" of the study. By beginning with their interest areas, it gives us the opportunity to further develop these interests while stretching into other areas of the outline as they increase their topic knowledge.

By working on a unit study for five or six weeks at a time, you can catch the children's attention and hold it for valuable learning. I try to wrap up each unit study in five or six weeks, whether or not we have "completed" the unit outline. The areas of the outline that we did not yet cover may be covered the next time we delve into the unit study topic (in a few months or perhaps next year). These guides are <u>non-consumable</u>—you can use them over and over again, covering new areas of interest as you review the previous things learned in the process.

The <u>Reading</u> and <u>Reference Lists</u> are lists of resources that feed right into various areas of the <u>Outline</u>. The books are listed with grade level recommendations and all the information that you need to locate them in the library or from your favorite book retailer. You can also order them through the national Inter-Library Loan System (I.L.L.)—check with the reference librarian at your local library.

There are several other components that also support the unit study.

The <u>Spelling and Vocabulary Lists</u> identify words that apply directly to the unit study, and are broken down into both Upper and Lower Levels for use with several ages.

The <u>Suggested Software, Games and Videos Lists</u> includes games, software and videos that make the learning fun, while reinforcing some of the basic concepts studied.

The <u>Activities and Field Trip Lists</u> include specific activity materials and field trip ideas that can be used with this unit to give some hands-on learning experience.

The <u>Internet Resources List</u> identifies sites that you might find helpful with this unit. The Internet is a wonderful resource to use with unit studies providing the sights and sounds of things that you might never otherwise experience! You can see works of art in the Louvre. See the sunrise on Mt. Rushmore, hear the sounds of the seashore and find many other things that will help provide an "immersion" in the unit study topic, as never before, without ever leaving home. As with any resource, use it with care and be there with the students as they go exploring new learning opportunities.

The author and the publisher care about you and your family. While not all of the materials recommended in this guide are written from a Christian perspective, they all have great educational value. Please use caution when using any materials. It's important to take the time to review books, games, and Internet sites before your children use them to make sure they meet your family's expectations.

As you can see, all of these sections have been included to help you build your unit study into a fun and fruitful learning adventure. Unit studies provide an excellent learning tool and give the students lifelong memories about the topic and the study.

Lots of phone numbers and addresses have been included to assist you in locating specific books and resources. To the best of our knowledge, all of these numbers were correct at the time of printing.

The left-hand pages of this book have been left "almost" blank for your notes, resources, ideas, children's artwork, or diagrams from this study or for ideas that you might like to pursue the next time you venture into this unit.

"Have fun & Enjoy the Adventure!"

Table of Contents

Introduction

The smell of the freshly turned earth, the new seed catalogs arriving in the mail and the singing of the returning birds—all are signs of the arrival of gardening season in many homes. There is something so basic and satisfying in the planting and nurturing of a garden, whether in a planned spot in the yard, in containers on a tiny balcony or on a bedroom window sill.

The joy and excitement on the children's faces as we begin to plan the garden and buy the seeds and begin to work in the soil—what motivation to keep us all moving and learning! These fun times together are still shared, even as the children grow older, and this is a wonderful blessing to families everywhere. From the first chance to look at how seeds sprout, how to compost (even indoors!), and then on to plant propagation and crop rotation—these are some of the concepts that we share with our students. We adjust and learning with them as they progress with their interests in plants.

This unit study has been developed to include the following topics:

🌹 Planning and planting your own garden
🌹 Plant science
🌹 History of gardens
🌹 Famous gardens
🌹 Famous scientists and gardeners

From developing, planting and maintaining our own garden and plant experiments through the study of gardens, their history and gardeners like Thomas Jefferson and Monet—all contribute to an EXCITING unit study. It is one that we will repeat on a regular basis at our house. There are plenty of topics and resources for all ages, and this study can keep your family busy for many seasons to come. We have both spring and autumn gardens at our house in Florida, as well as various flower gardens and indoor plants. The knowledge that we have all gained from our studies has been amazing.

It is so rewarding to see how much our children have learned and how self-sufficient they are becoming. They look forward to planning their own gardens and selecting the plants that they want to experiment with—this is a self-motivated interest that they will probably carry throughout their lives. This is a measurement of true success, according to our way of thinking! Enjoy the adventure and get planting!

Unit Study Outline

I. Introduction to Gardens

A. Definition of a garden

B. Gardens and their role in history
1. Garden of Eden
2. Garden of Gethsemane
3. Gardens throughout the Bible
4. Gardens in later civilizations

C. Gardens around the world

D. Uses of gardens
1. Provide food, herbs and flowers
2. Provide a source of pleasure
3. Provide a place of beauty and relaxation to enjoy many kinds of plants and animals

E. Elements of a garden appeal to the senses
1. Sight—visually appealing through the beauty of the plants, the garden layout and other elements
2. Smell—the various scents of the plants and their fruit and flowers, and the smells of the tilled soil
3. Taste—enjoying the produce fresh from the garden
4. Sound—hearing the noises of the animal inhabitants (croaking toads, buzzing bees), as well as the sound of water running through a fountain or tinkling wind chimes
5. Touch—feeling the various textures of the many plants and their components, as well as feeling the soil itself

II. Types of Gardens

A. Rose garden

B. Flower garden

C. Vegetable garden

D. Victory garden

E. Kitchen garden

F. Oriental garden

G. Rock garden

H. Formal garden

I. Herb garden

J.   Botanical garden

K.   Container garden

L.   Experimental garden

III. History of Gardens

A.   Beginning of time—Garden of Eden

B.   Spread of domestic crop plants throughout history

    1.   Early trade routes developed for trade of spices and herbs

    2.   Monks in medieval times developed herb gardens and studied herbal medicine

    3.   New World exploration

        a.   Early colonists learned about corn and crops for North America from the Indians

        b.   Explorers returned to Europe with many different types of plants and seeds from the new world

C.   Gardens throughout time have usually been tended primarily by women—men were usually responsible for the tilling and soil preparation, and then the women took over, planting, weeding and maintaining the garden for the family

D.   Gardens had value for growing medicines for the family—herbs were believed to be the basis of their health and were added to the evening meal, which might be soup with plenty of herbs which helped to prevent various ailments

E.   Famous American gardens

    1.   Monticello—Thomas Jefferson

    2.   Mount Vernon—George Washington

    3.   The Hermitage—Andrew Jackson

    4.   White House Gardens

    5.   Winterthur in Delaware

    6.   National Arboretum in Washington, D.C.

        a.   Early American Garden

        b.   American Indian Garden

IV. Basic Plant Science

A.   Plants form the base of the food chain, taking in inorganic elements and using them to produce organic compounds

B.   Some interesting fields of plant science that apply to gardens
    1.   Botany
    2.   Horticulture
    3.   Agriculture
C.   Uses of plants
    1.   Provide food
        a.   Vegetables
        b.   Fruit
        c.   Herbs and spices
    2.   Provide medicines (quinine, digitalis)
    3.   Provide elements for our shelter (wood)
    4.   Provide energy resources (wood, fossil fuel)
    5.   Provide clothing elements (cotton, flax)
D.   Plant science and structure (botany)
    1.   Plant classification (taxonomy)
        a.   Flowering division
        b.   Nonflowering division
    2.   Differences in plants and animals
        a.   Cell structure (this is a good time to introduce the use of a microscope, if possible)
        b.   Food requirements
        c.   Food for plant growth is manufactured by a process called photosynthesis, utilizing chlorophyll
    3.   Basic plant structure
        a.   Roots
            (1)   Fibrous root system
            (2)   Tap root system
        b.   Stem
            (1)   Types of stems
                (a)   Woody
                (b)   Herbaceous
            (2)   Circulatory system
                (a)   Xylem tissue
                (b)   Phloem tissue
        c.   Leaf
            (1)   Leaf Blade
                (a)   Leaf base
                (b)   Midrib
                (c)   Margin
                (d)   Vein

     (2) Petiole

     (3) Apex

   d. Flower

     (1) Petal

     (2) Sepal

     (3) Stamen

     (4) Pollen

     (5) Stigma

     (6) Pistil

     (7) Ovule

   e. Seed

     (1) Seed coat

     (2) Embryo

     (3) Cotyledon

     (4) Endosperm

 E. Plant requirements

  1. Water

  2. Air

  3. Nutrients

  4. Sunshine

 F. Geography and plants

  1. Different areas of the world can support various plants

  2. Zones have been named for these land areas of the world

   a. Desert

   b. Forest

   c. Grassland

   d. Mountain

   e. Rainforest

   f. Tropic

   g. Tundra

  3. The U.S. Department of Agriculture has developed hardiness zones for the United States, based on minimum temperatures for each zone (usually displayed in American seed catalogs)

V. Your own garden

 A. Locate the garden, and consider these important factors

  1. Daily hours of sunlight

  2. Good drainage

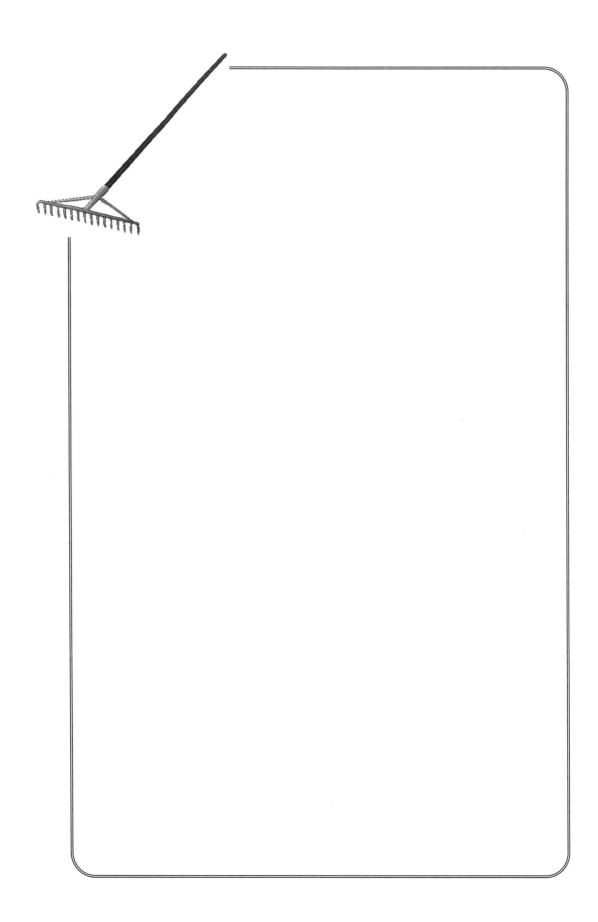

3.   Soil quality
4.   Water availability
5.   Wind protection
B.   Plan the garden
   1.   Determine the space available for the garden
   2.   Consider crops that grow well in your area
      a.   Climate
      b.   Season
      c.   Soil quality
   3.   Design different gardens for different seasons
      a.   Cool weather crops
      b.   Warm weather crops
   4.   Popular home garden plants
      a.   Vegetables
         (1)   Tomatoes
         (2)   Green beans
         (3)   Peas
         (4)   Cucumbers
         (5)   Radishes
         (6)   Carrots
         (7)   Squash
         (8)   Pumpkins
         (9)   Watermelon
       (10)   Eggplant
       (11)   Onions
       (12)   Potatoes
       (13)   Strawberries
       (14)   Lettuce
       (15)   Peppers
      b.   Herbs
         (1)   Mint
         (2)   Oregano
         (3)   Sweet basil
         (4)   Chives
         (5)   Parsley
         (6)   Dill
         (7)   Rosemary
      c.   Flowers
         (1)   Marigolds
         (2)   Zinnias

          (3)   Sunflowers

          (4)   Pansies

          (5)   Petunias

          (6)   Impatiens

          (7)   Snapdragons

          (8)   Sweet peas

C.   Prepare the soil

    1.   Till and remove rocks, roots and other debris

    2.   Test a sample of the soil to determine the chemistry of your soil at the garden site

        a.   Testing is usually available through the County Extension service

        b.   Use soil test results and add ingredients to the soil to improve the fertility and adjust the chemistry, if needed

    3.   Add nutrients to the soil to enrich the organic matter content

        a.   Compost

        b.   Fertilizer

D.   Plant the garden

    1.   Seeds

    2.   Seedlings

        a.   Purchase at local nurseries

        b.   Purchase through plant and seed catalogs

        c.   Start in your home from seed

    3.   Bulbs

E.   Maintain the garden

    1.   Feed

        a.   Fertilize

        b.   Compost

    2.   Water

        a.   Rain

        b.   Irrigation

    3.   Insects in the garden

        a.   Helpful insects

            (1)   Earthworms

            (2)   Bees

            (3)   Ladybugs

            (4)   Praying mantises

b.   Harmful insects
       (1)   Beetles
       (2)   Caterpillars
       (3)   Aphids
c.   Controlling harmful insects
       (1)   Natural methods
       (2)   Chemical methods
d.   Other considerations
       (1)   Birds
       (2)   Small animals (rabbits, raccoons)
4.   Weeding/mulching
     a.   Weeding helps make certain that nutrients and water are used by crops, instead of weeds
     b.   Mulching helps to minimize weed growth and conserve soil moisture and many different materials can be used
       (1)   Shredded wood bark
       (2)   Newspaper
       (3)   Plastic sheets
       (4)   Leaves
       (5)   Compost

F.   Harvest the garden's produce
1.   Pick crops when ripe
2.   Enjoy the produce fresh
3.   Preserve the produce
     a.   Canning
     b.   Freezing
     c.   Drying

VI.   Famous scientists, gardeners and planters

A.   Gregor Mendel
B.   George Washington Carver
C.   Thomas Jefferson
D.   Monet (Claude Monet)
E.   John Chapman (Johnny Appleseed)

VII. Art and gardens

   A. Famous artists that painted gardens and natural elements
      1. Monet (Claude Monet)
         a. *The Artist's Garden at Giverny*
         b. *Women in the Garden*
         c. *The Artist's Garden at Vétheuil*
         d. *Water Lilies*
      2. Beatrix Potter
      3. Vincent Van Gogh
      4. Auguste Renoir
   B. Still life paintings of garden produce
   C. Nature sketches in garden settings

VIII. Poetry and gardens

   A. *A Child's Garden of Verses*, by Robert Louis Stevenson
      1. "The Flowers"
      2. "The Gardener"
      3. "Summer Sun"
      4. "Farewell to the Farm"
   B. *The Door at the End of Our Garden,* by Frederick Weatherly

Spelling and Vocabulary

Lower Level

bean

herb

plant

grow

row

dig

dry

wet

dirt

soil

pot

green

glove

stem

leaf

root

thin

climb

pole

vine

care

food

fruit

vegetable

hoe

weed

water

mulch

till

watch

prepare

harvest

pick

cage

tie

runner

peel

husk

stalk

bulb

color

can

label

plan

sketch

string

inch

measure

seed

seedling

tomato

corn

peas

carrot

squash

radish

watermelon

cucumber

pumpkin

flower

Spelling and Vocabulary

Upper Level

cultivate
botany
plant
science
gardening
fertilizer
planning
rotation
vegetable
pollination

tomato
potato
cucumber
radish
lettuce
squash
avocado
watermelon
cantaloupe
strawberry

chlorophyll
photosynthesis
nutrient
germination
pollen
temperature
carbon dioxide
oxygen
sunlight
development

herbs
rosemary
thyme
oregano
basil
dill
chives
mint
parsley
sage

embryo
embryology
seed coat
cotyledon
endosperm
pistil
stamen
stigma
annual
perennial

horticulture
agriculture
hybrid
transplant
genetics
propagate
medicinal
insecticide
organic
composting

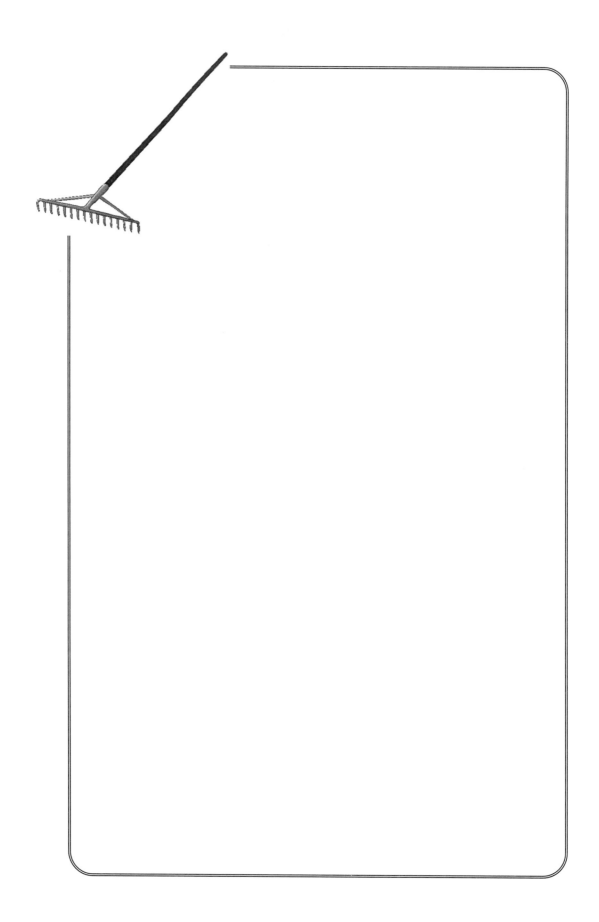

Writing Ideas

Here are some ideas to help incorporate writing in a unit study. Choose one or two and watch what happens!

1. Have the children write letters to some of the seed companies listed in the Activities Section. Let them compose their own letters and request information for a study on seeds and gardens. They can write the letters themselves or dictate them to a parent or older sibling.

2. Plan to have each student keep a journal of his garden adventures. For older children, have them record the garden work they have completed each day, the plan for tomorrow's work and sketches of the garden, plants or insects that they observe. Younger children can keep a journal of sketches about their work in the garden each day.

3. For the older students, consider having them compare your garden and efforts to those of pioneers like Laura Ingalls Wilder or others that they have studied. They could write about the differences in tools, seeds, plant varieties, fertilizers, etc., as well as writing about the likenesses in these areas.

4. If your children have grandparents or other relatives that cannot stop by and see the garden in person, consider asking your students to write weekly letters. Have them describe the garden activities to the distant friends or relatives, using words to paint a picture of the garden, instead of using drawings. At the end of the garden season, have the children send some pictures to the same people. See if the letters described the garden as the photographs show it.

5. Some of the scientific names of the various plants used in the garden are fun to study. Look up the meanings of the various parts of the words in a good unabridged dictionary. An older student could research the formal name for a particular garden plant, including its origin and meaning, and then prepare an oral or written report on his plant.

General Activity Resources

Activities provide a great way to reinforce the material that we learn in a unit study. They provide important hands-on learning. We have fun and are challenged at the same time. There are numerous activity books available about gardening and plant science at most libraries, and your family will probably come up with some fun activities of their own. Here are a few activity resources to get you started:

The Botany Coloring Book, by Paul Young. For grades 7 - 12. Published by HarperCollins. Available from: Farm Country General Store, Rte. 1, Box 63, Metamora, IL 61548. (800) 551-3276.

The Amazing Potato Book, The Amazing Apple Book, and **The Amazing Dirt Book,** all by Paulette Bourgeois. Published by Addison-Wesley, 1 Jacob Way, Reading, MA 01867. (800) 447-2226. Available from: Farm Country General Store, Rte. 1, Box 63, Metamora, IL 61548. (800) 551-3276.

Martin House Gourd Seeds Kit, produced by the Purple Martin Conservation Association, providing seeds, growing instructions and gourd preparation. Available from Nature's Workshop, 22777 State Road 119, Goshen, IN 46526-9375. (800) 824-2329.

Flower & Leaf Presses, a complete selection available through Mountain View Books, Rte.. 1, Box 1020, Elizabethton, TN 37643. (615) 542-3374.

Green Thumbs: A Kid's Activity Guide to Indoor and Outdoor Gardening, by Laurie Carlson. Grades Pre-K - 4. Published by Chicago Review Press, 814 N. Franklin Street, Chicago, IL 60610. Available from Farm Country General Store, (800) 551-3276.

Coloring books from Dover Publishing, 31 East 2nd Street, Mineola, NY 11501. Great for Grades 3 and up:

American Wildflowers
Favorite Roses
Garden Flowers
Herbs
House Plants
Old Fashioned Farm Life

Science Activity Resources

Here are some activity-oriented science resources that work well with this unit study. There are many types of activities included for all ages—try to select a few that would appeal to your family.

GREEN THUMBS: Corn and Beans, by Ron Marson. (TOPS Learning Systems Series, #39). Grades 3-10. Published by TOPS Learning Systems, 10970 S. Mulino Rd., Canby, OR 97013.

Soil Test Kit, by Rapitest. This resource could be used for a great science project in soil chemistry. It includes up to 40 different tests. Available from Nature's Workshop, 22777 State Road 119, Goshen, IN 46526-9375. (800) 824-2329.

PLANTS: Investigations in Science, by June Hetzel, Susan Miller and Brenda Wyma. Grades 4-8. Published by Creative Teaching Press, Inc. Available through Education Works, 35 Shaw Street, New London, CT 06320. (203) 443-9666.

Botany Projects for Young Scientists, by Maurice Bleifeld. Grades 9-12. Published by Franklin Watts, 5450 Cumberland Ave., Chicago, IL 60656. (800) 672-6672.

Science With Plants, by Mike Unwin. (Usborne Science Activities). Grades 1-4. Published by EDC Publishing, 10302 E. 55th Place, Tulsa, OK 74146.

Botany: Forty-Nine More Science Fair Projects, by Robert Bonnet and Daniel Keen. Grades 4-7. Published by TAB Books, distributed by McGraw Hill, P.O. Box 40, Blue Ridge Summit, PA 17294. (800) 822-8158.

Plants & Seeds: Through the Microscope, by John Stidworthy. Grades 4-6. Published by Franklin Watts, 5450 Cumberland Ave., Chicago, IL 60656. (800) 672-6672.

Backyard Scientist: Exploring Earthworms with Me, by Jane Hoffman. Grades Pre-K-6. Published by Backyard Scientist, P.O. Box 16966, Irvine, CA 92713. (714) 551-2392.

Seeds to Plants: Projects with Biology, by Jeffrey Bates. (Hands on Science Series) Grades 5-9. Published by Franklin Watts, 5450 Cumberland Ave., Chicago, IL 60656. (800) 672-6672.

Thirty-Nine Easy Plant Biology Experiments, by Robert Wood. (Science for Kids Series) Grades 7 and up. Published by TAB Books, P.O. Box 40, Blue Ridge Summit, PA 17294. (800) 822-8158.

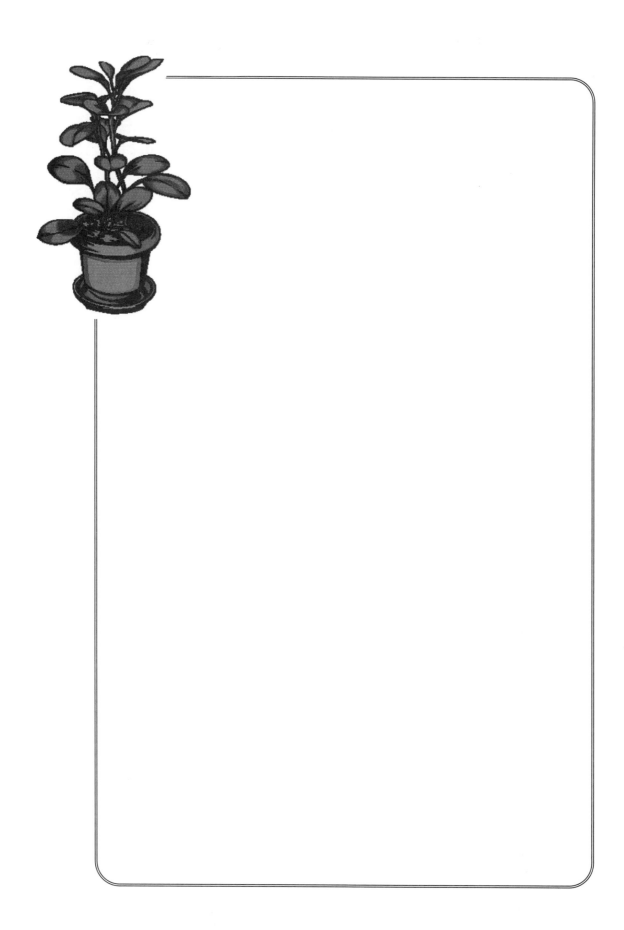

General Educational Resources

There are so many helpful places to write for educational resources about gardening and food preparation. Here are a few of them:

Office of Public Affairs
Department of Agriculture
74th St. & Independence Ave., SW
Washington, DC 20250

National Gardening Association
180 Flynn Ave.
Burlington, VT 05401

For more information on preserving the crops from your family garden, write to:

Ball Corporation
Consumer Products Division
345 S. High St.
Muncie, IN 47305

You can develop a collection of materials on gardening by writing or having the students write away for information. Seed and plant companies and large nurseries may have catalogs or information to provide for a unit study on gardens. Here are some of the main companies, their addresses and phone numbers:

Park Seed Company
Cokesbury Rd.
North Greenwood, SC 29646
(800) 845-3369

Wayside Gardens
P.O. Box 1
Hodges, SC 29695-0001
(800) 845-1124

W. Atlee Burpee Company
300 Park Ave.
Warminster, PA 18974
(800) 888-1447

Thompson & Morgan
P.O. Box 1308
Jackson, NJ 08527
(800) 274-7333

Jackson & Perkins
P.O. Box 1028
Medford, OR 97501
(800) 292-4769

Nichols Garden Nursery
1190 North Pacific Hwy.
Albany, OR 97321
(503) 928-9280

Job Opportunities

Here is a list of some of the jobs that involve gardens and plants. There are others that I'm sure you will identify, but these are some of the main ones that we investigated during our unit study.

Botanist

Wholesale florist

Biologist

Arborist

Farmer

Grounds keeper/manager

Agricultural engineer

Interior landscaping

County extension agent

Floral designer

Landscape architect

Horticultural therapist

Plant taxonomist

Landscape contractor

Horticulturalist

Soil scientist

Ornamental horticulturalist

Retail florist

Forest ranger

Nursery worker/owner

Entomologist

Gardener

For more information about these jobs or others that may be interesting, go to the reference librarian in the public library and ask for publications on careers. Some that might be helpful include:

The Encyclopedia of Careers and Vocational Guidance,
published by J. G. Ferguson Publishing Company, Chicago.

Occupational Outlook Handbook, published by the US Department of Labor, Bureau of Labor Statistics. It presents detailed information on 250 occupations that employ the vast majority of workers. It describes the nature of the work, training and educational requirements, working conditions and earnings potential.

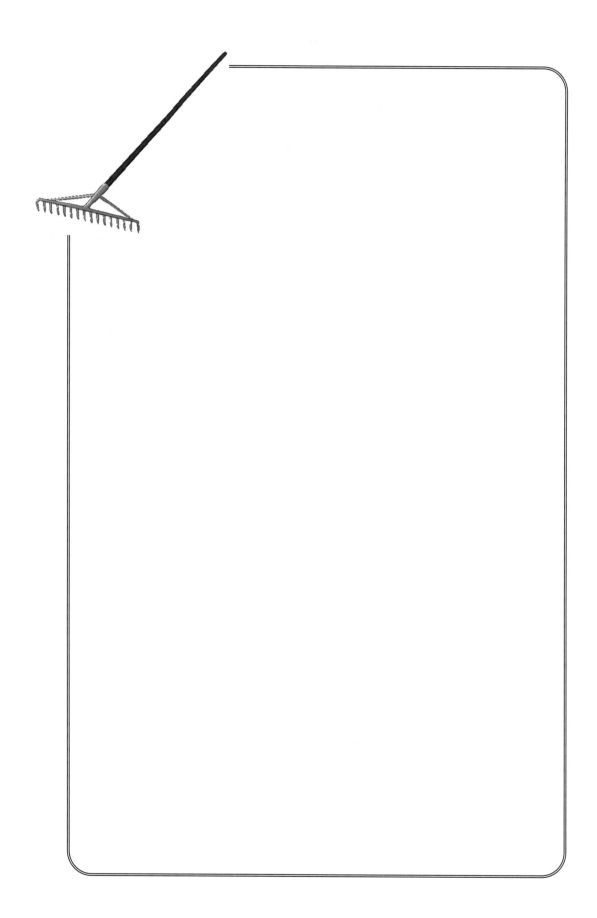

Room Decorations

When working on a unit study, we try to decorate the room with items that relate to our current topic of interest. This allows the students to see the important information on a regular basis and provides a place to view their work. For gardens, consider some of the following ideas:

1. Visit a local nursery or botanical garden and collect brochures and posters that might be helpful during the unit study. Have the students enlarge some of the drawings for a wall display.

2. Have your students develop a poster-size wall diagram of their planned garden. They should indicate crops and locations, while keeping the drawing to scale.

3. As the students plan and plant the garden, take photos of the progress. Mount the pictures on a poster on the wall, along with the date of each picture—it is rewarding for them to see how the landscape changed so quickly, along with the fruits of their labors!

4. Consider having the children try their hand at bonsai and house plants for your study room. There are numerous books available on these topics, and the indoor gardening projects make great decorations long after the unit study has been completed.

5. Give the children some graph paper and a long measuring tape. Have them develop a large scale drawing of your yard, including trees, gardens and other landscape features.

6. As you study the different parts of plants and their structures, have the students create some wall-sized diagrams of the plants that hold their interest.

Game, Video and Software Suggestions

Games provide a great way to reinforce the material that we learn. We have fun, while reviewing important information and concepts around the kitchen table or on the computer. The games, videos and software listed are just a sample of what is available. Make sure to check with your local library, software store and video rental store for other titles that your family might enjoy using with this unit.

GAMES:

Don't Bug Me, a fun board game for grades K-3. Published by Aristoplay, P.O. Box 7529, Ann Arbor, Michigan 48107. (800) 634-7738. Available from The Home School Books & Supplies, 104 S. West Ave., Arlington, WA 98223. (800) 788-1221.

The Pollination Game, a card game for grades 2 and up. Published by Ampersand Press, 8040 N.E. Day Rd. West #5-A, Bainbridge Island, WA 98110. (800) 624-4263. Available from The Home School Books & Supplies, 104 S. West Ave., Arlington, WA 98223. (800) 788-1221.

The Farming Game, a great game that teaches some of the business and economic principles of raising crops. Grades 5 and up. Available from Farm Country General Store, Rte.. 1, Box 63, Metamora, IL 61548 (800) 551-3276.

VIDEOS:

The Power in Plants, by Moody Science Adventures, using spectacular time-lapse photography, this video reveals the mysterious mechanisms behind plant life. Available from Great Christian Books. (800) 775-5422.

Power Plants, by Moody Institute of Science, laugh and learn as the Power Plant Kids and zany Professor Schnaegel explore the world of plants, Available from Great Christian Books. (800) 775-5422.

The Secret Garden, several versions available on video

SOFTWARE:

Garden Encyclopedia from Books That Work, **Garden Companion** from lifestyle Software Group, and **Complete Guide to Gardening** from Better Homes & Gardens and Multicom Publishing—all on CD-ROM and fun to use when planning your own gardens. Go see a demonstration of these and many other software packages on gardening through many computer software stores.

SimFarm, an exciting farm simulation game that teaches the fundamentals of farming crops as well as raising livestock. Ages 8 and up—great fun for the whole family. Published by MAXIS, 2 Theatre Square, Orinda, CA 94563-3346. (510) 254-9700. Also available through many computer software stores.

Field Trip Ideas

There are so many field trips that can be enjoyed while learning about gardens and plants, that it is hard to list all of the ones that you might want to consider. Here are some ideas to get you started!

1. If there is a nearby pick-your-own farm, try to have an outing to watch some of the work that takes place throughout the growing season. From initial planting through harvesting, the children will learn by watching and participating in this large-scale "garden" operation.

2. Plan a visit to your County Agriculture Extension office or State Agricultural office. Explain that you are working on a study about gardens and plant science. They usually have a wealth of free informational books and pamphlets about gardening in your area, as well as 4-H literature available for all ages. Some extension agencies offer workshops on gardening for all ages, and these can be fun to attend as a family. (If you have difficulty locating phone numbers for these offices, contact your local librarian. They should have complete government phone number listings.)

3. Check with your local library or Chamber of Commerce to locate any arboretums and botanical gardens in your area. They usually offer guided tours. Some are focused on children and their observations.

4. Many areas have active garden clubs that hold seasonal displays or shows for many types of plants, including orchids, roses, etc. The shows are very informative and your family might come away inspired to try a hand at new kinds of plants for your own home.

5. If you have a relative or family friend that has a working farm, you might consider taking your students there to spend some time and observe the work as well as lend a hand. They will have a great time as well as learn volumes and make some lifetime memories.

6. Visit a local food processing facility to observe how commercially grown crops are preserved. These might include a fruit grove processing plant, a canning factory, a juicing factory and others.

7. We also have enjoyed going on regular visits to the local farmers' market. We use the opportunity to compare their produce to that from our own garden. They have a broad variety of plants and are usually more than willing to answer all of the children's questions.

Subject Word List

A list of SUBJECT search words has been included to help with this unit. To find material about gardens, go to your library's card catalog and/or computer and look up:

agriculture
botanical classification
botanical gardens
botany
farming
food crops
fruit
garden
gardening
greenhouse
herbs
homesteading
horticulture
landscape
ornamental horticulture
plant genetics
plant propagation
plants
plant science
soil chemistry
taxonomy
vegetables

George Washington Carver
John Chapman
Thomas Jefferson
Gregor Mendel
Claude Monet
Beatrix Potter
Auguste Renoir
Vincent Van Gogh

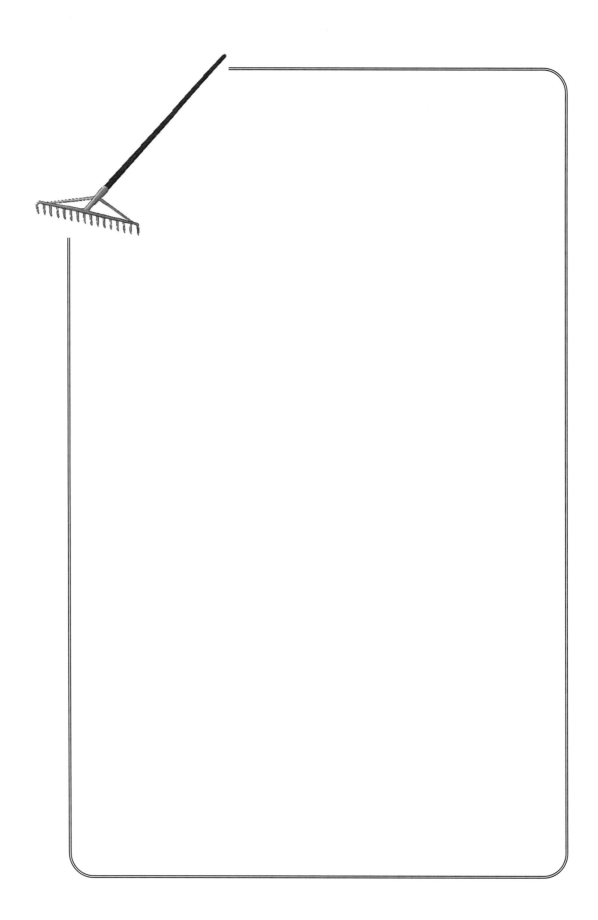

Trivia Questions

1. During which war did many Americans plant victory gardens?

2. What pioneer set out for the west, preaching and planting apple trees along the way for other pioneers?

3. Which garden vegetable is actually a fruit, and was once considered poisonous?

4. An Austrian monk was the first person to discover the basic principles of genetics and heredity. What was his name?

5. What garden plant did Gregor Mendel use for his experiments?

6. What did the Indians teach the Pilgrims to use for fertilizer in their gardens?

7. What do the three numbers mean that are used to describe commercial fertilizers?

8. What is the difference between a monocot and a dicot?

9.   What are the three main classifications of natural objects here on Earth?

10.   Who introduced the use of binomial plant names in 1753?

Trivia Answers

1. During which war did many Americans plant victory gardens?
    World War II

2. What pioneer set out for the west, preaching and planting apple trees along the way for other pioneers?
    John Chapman, also known as Johnny Appleseed

3. Which garden vegetable is actually a fruit, and was once considered poisonous?
    Tomato

4. An Austrian monk was the first person to discover the basic principles of genetics and heredity. What was his name?
    Born Johann Mendel, he later changed his name to Gregor when he entered the monastery

5. What garden plant did Gregor Mendel use for his experiments?
    Garden Pea

6. What did the Indians teach the Pilgrims to use for fertilizer in their gardens?
    Fish

7. What do the three numbers mean that are used to describe commercial fertilizers?
    The first number indicates the percentage of nitrogen, the second number represents the percentage of phosphate and the third number indicates the percentage of potassium

8. What is the difference between a monocot and a dicot?
    A monocot is a plant that has one cotyledon (seed leaves of an embryo plant) while a dicot is a plant that has two cotyledons

9. What are the three main classifications of natural objects here on Earth?
    The plant kingdom, the animal kingdom and the mineral kingdom

10. Who introduced the use of binomial plant names in 1753?
    Carolus Linnaeus

History Resources

Gardens of the Middle Ages, by Marilyn Stokstad and Jerry Stanard. Grades 9 and up. Published by Spencer Museum of Art, University of Kansas, Lawrence, KS 66045. (913) 864-4710.

Farm Through the Ages, by Philip Steele. Grades 3-6. Published by Troll Associates, 100 Corporate Dr., Mahwah, NJ 07430. (800) 526-5289.

Baker Encyclopedia of Bible Plants: Flowers & Trees, Fruits & Vegetables, Ecology, by Nigel Hepper. Grades 8 and up. Published by Baker Books, P.O. Box 6287, Grand Rapids, MI 49516. (800) 877-2665.

Egyptian Farmers, by James Kerr. (Beginning History Series). Grades 2-5. Published by Franklin Watts, 5450 Cumberland Ave., Chicago, IL 60656. (800) 672-6672.

Thomas Jefferson's Garden Book, by Edwin Betts. (Memoirs Series, Volume 22). Young Adults--Grades 9 and up. Published by American Philosophical Society, 104 S. Fifth St., Philadelphia, PA 19106. (215) 440-3400.

Colonial American Home Life, by John Warner. Grades 5-8. Published by Franklin Watts, 5450 Cumberland Ave., Chicago, IL 60656. (800) 672-6672.

Food for the Settler, by Bobbie Kalman. (Early Settler Life Series) Grades 4-5. Published by Crabtree Publishing, 350 Fifth Avenue, Suite 3308, New York, NY 10118. (800) 387-7650.

Gardens on Paper: Prints & Drawings, 1200-1900, by Virginia Clayton. Grades 9 and up. Published by the National Gallery of Art, Fourth St. and Constitution Ave. N.W., Washington, DC 20565. Thomas Jefferson's Flower Garden at Monticello, by Edwin Betts and Hazelhurst Perkins. Grades 9 and up. Published by University Press of Virginia, P.O. Box 3608, University Station, Charlottesville, VA 22903. (804) 924-3468.

The Gardens and Grounds at Mt. Vernon: How George Washington Planned & Planted Them, by Elizabeth DeForest. Grades 9 and up. Published by University Press of Virginia, P.O. Box 3608, University Station, Charlottesville, VA 22903. (804) 924-3468.

Plant Science Resources

Plant Science, by Anita Ganeri. (Science Questions & Answers Series). Grades 5 and up. Published by Simon & Schuster, owners of Macmillan Children's Books, 200 Old Tappan Rd., Old Tappan, NJ 07675. (800) 223-2348.

Plants: A Creative Hands-on Approach to Science, by Wendy Baker and Andrew Haslam. (Make It Work! Series). Grades 2-5. Published by Simon & Schuster, owners of Macmillan Children's Books, 200 Old Tappan Rd., Old Tappan, NJ 07675. (800) 223-2348.

Studying Plants, a Milliken Science Transparency Reproducible Book . Grades 4-9. Published by Milliken Publishing Company, 1100 Research Blvd., St. Louis, MO 63132.

A Handbook of Nature Study, by Anna Comstock. Grades 5-12. Published by Cornell University Press, Sage House, 512 East State Street, Ithaca, NY 14850. Available from Greenleaf Press, 1570 Old LaGuardo Rd., Lebanon, TN 37087. (615) 449-1617.

From Flower to Fruit, by Anne Dowden. Grades 3 and up. Published by Ticknor & Fields Books for Young Readers, Houghton Mifflin Company, Individuals/Trade Division, 181 Ballardvale Rd., Wilmington, MA 01887 (800) 225- 3362; Schools Division, 1900 S. Batavia Ave., Geneva, IL 60134 (800) 323-5663.

The Flower, Classic Studies in Science for the Young Mind. Grades 3-6. Published by Bee Smart. Available from God's World, P.O. Box 2330, Asheville, NC 28802. (800) 951-2665.

From Seed to Plant, by Gail Gibbons. Grades PreK-3. Published by Holiday, 425 Madison Avenue, New York, NY 10017. (212) 688-0085.

Baker Encyclopedia of Bible Plants: Flowers & Trees, Fruits & Vegetables, Ecology, by Nigel Hepper. Grades 8 and up. Published by Baker Book House Co., P.O. Box 6287, Grand Rapids, MI 49516. (800) 877-2665.

The Visual Dictionary of Plants (Eyewitness Visual Dictionaries Series) Grades 4 and up. Published by Dorling Kindersley. Distributed by Houghton Mifflin, Individuals/Trade Division, 181 Ballardvale Rd., Wilmington, MA 01887 (800) 225-3362; Schools Division, 1900 S. Batavia Ave., Geneva, IL 60134 (800) 323 5663.

Science with Plants, by Mike Unwin. (Usborne Science Activities). Grades 1-4. Published by EDC Publishing, 10302 E. 55th Place, Tulsa, OK 74146.

Usborne First Book of Nature, by Rosamund Cox, Barbara Cork and Ruth Thomson. Grades 1- 5. Published by EDC Publishing, 10302 E. 55th Place, Tulsa, OK 74146.

Usborne Mysteries & Marvels of Plant Life, by Barbara Cork. Grades 2-5. Published by EDC Publishing, 10302 E. 55th Place, Tulsa, OK 74146.

Plants & Seeds Through the Microscope, by John Stidworthy. Grades 4-6. Published by Franklin Watts, 5450 Cumberland Ave., Chicago, IL 60656. (800)672-6672.

The Life Cycle of a Sunflower, by Philip Parker. Grades 2-4. Published by Franklin Watts, 5450 Cumberland Ave., Chicago, IL 60656. (800) 672-6672.

Plant Families, by Carol Lerner. Grades 4 and up. Published by Morrow Junior Books, 1350 Avenue of the Americas, New York, NY 10019. (212) 261-6691.

Growing Plants, by Barbara Taylor. (Fun With Simple Science Series). Grades 2-4. Published by Franklin Watts, 5450 Cumberland Ave., Chicago, IL 60656. (800) 672-6672.

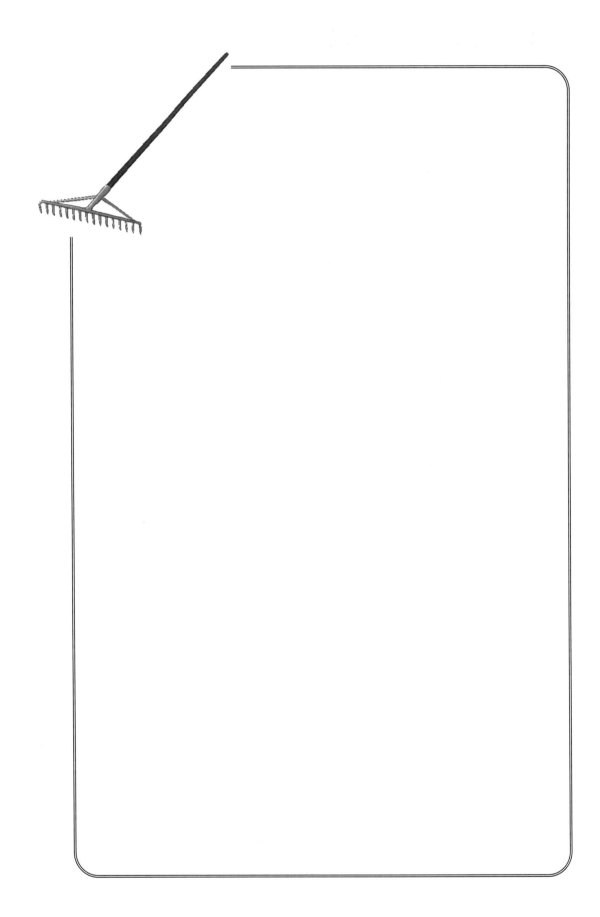

General Gardening Resources

Best Kids Garden Book, by the Sunset Editors. Grades 2-6. Published by Sunset Publishing, Menlo Park, CA 94025. (800) 227-7346.

The Victory Garden Kids' Book, by Marjorie Waters. Grades 4-8. Published by The Globe Pequot Press, P.O. Box 833, Old Saybrook, CT 06475. (800) 243-0495.

Kids' Gardening: A Kids' Guide to Messing Around in the Dirt, by Kevin & Kim Raftery. Grades K-4. Published by Klutz Press, 2121 Staunton Ct., Palo Alto, CA 94306. (415) 857-0888.

Green Thumbs: A Kid's Activity Guide to Indoor and Outdoor Gardening, by Laurie Carlson. Grades Pre-K-4. Published by Chicago Review Press, 814 N. Franklin Street, Chicago, IL 60610. Available from Farm Country General Store, (800) 551-3276.

Look at Seeds & Weeds, by Rena Kirkpatrick. (Look at Science Series). Grades 2-4. Published by Raintree Steck-Vaughn, P.O. Box 26015, Austin, TX 78755. (800) 531-5015.

Plant Families, by Carol Lerner. Grades 4 and up. Published by Morrow Junior Books, 1350 Avenue of the Americas, New York, NY 10019. (212) 261-6691.

How Do Apples Grow?, by Betsy Maestro. Grades K-4. (Let's Read & Find Out Science Books). Published by HarperCollins Children's Books, 1000 Keystone Industrial Park, Scranton, PA 18512. (800) 242-7737.

Fruit, by Pascale DeBourgoing. (First Discovery Books) Grades PreK-2. Published by Scholastic, Inc., P.O. Box 7502, Jefferson City, MO 65201. (800) 325-6149.

Vegetables, by Susan Wake. Grades 1-4. (Foods We Eat Series). Published by Carolrhoda Books, Inc., 241 First Ave. N., Minneapolis, MN 55401. (800) 328-4929.

Back to Basics: How to Learn and Enjoy Traditional American Skills, published by Reader's Digest Association, Inc., Pleasantville, NY.

The Kitchen Gardeners' Guide: Time-Tested Advice on How to Plan, Prepare, Grow and Harvest a Bountiful Family Vegetable Garden, edited by Donald J. Berg. Grades 9 and up. Published by Ten Speed Press, P.O. Box 7123, Berkeley, CA 94707.

Gardening With The Experts: Vegetable Gardens, by Mary Moody. Grades 8 and up. Published by Harlaxton Publishing, United Kingdom. ISBN 1-85837-035-3.

Famous Scientists, Gardeners and Planters Resources

The Story of George Washington Carver, by Eva Moore. Grades 2-5. Published by Scholastic, Inc., P.O. Box 7502, Jefferson City, MO 65102. (800) 325-6149.

Tom Jefferson: Third President of the U.S., by Helen A. Monsell. Grades 2-6. (Childhood of Famous Americans Series). Published by Simon & Schuster, owners of Macmillan Children's Books, 200 Old Tappan Rd., Old Tappan, NJ 07675. (800) 223-2348.

Thomas Jefferson's Garden Book, by Edwin Betts. (Memoirs Series, Volume 22). Young Adults--Grades 9 and up. Published by American Philosophical Society, 104 S. Fifth St., Philadelphia, PA 19106. (215) 440-3400.

Johnny Appleseed-John Chapman: God's Faithful Planter, by David R. Collins. (The Sower Series). Grades 5 and up. Published by Mott Media, 1000 E. Huron, Milford, MI 48381. (810) 685-8773.

John Chapman: The Man Who was Johnny Appleseed, by Carol Green. (Rookie Biography Series). Grades K-3. Published by Children's Press, P.O. Box 1331, Danbury, CT 06813. (800) 621-1115.

Thomas Jefferson: Author, Inventor, President, by Carol Green. (Rookie Biography Series). Grades K-3. Published by Children's Press, P.O. Box 1331, Danbury, CT 06813. (800) 621-1115.

George Washington Carver: Scientist and Teacher, by Carol Green. (Rookie Biography Series). Grades K-3. Published by Children's Press, P.O. Box 1331, Danbury, CT 06813. (800) 621-1115.

Fine Arts Resources

Monet, Eyewitness Art Series. Grades 5 and up. Published by Dorling Kindersley. Distributed by Houghton Mifflin, Wayside Rd., Burlington, MA 01803. (800) 225-3362

What Makes a Monet a Monet?, by Richard Muhlberger. Grades 5 and up. Published by Viking Children's Books, 375 Hudson St., New York, NY 10014. (212) 366-2000.

MONET: An Introduction to the Artist's Life and Work, by Antony Mason. (Famous Artists Series). Grades 4 and up. Published by Barron's Educational Series, Inc., 250 Wireless Boulevard, Hauppauge, NY 11788. (800) 645-3476.

Beatrix Potter's Art, by Anne Stevenson Hobbs. Published by Warner, Division of Penguin Books, P.O. Box 120, Bergenfield, NJ 07621. (800) 526-0275.

Country Artist: A Story About Beatrix Potter, by David R. Collins. Grades 3-6. Published by Carolrhoda Books, Inc., 241 First Ave., N., Minneapolis, MN 55401.(800) 328-4929.

Artist's Gardens: From Claude Monet to Jennifer Bartlett, by Madison Cox. Grades 9 and up. Published by Abrams, Inc., 100 Fifth Ave., New York, NY 10011. (800) 345-1359.

Linnea in Monet's Garden, by Christina Bjork. Grades 3-6. Published by Farrar, Straus & Giroux, 19 Union Square West, New York, NY 10003. (800) 788-6262.

Monet's Garden: Through the Seasons at Giverny, by Vivian Russell. Grades 9 and up. Published by Stewart, Tabori & Chang, 575 Broadway, New York, NY 10012.

Miscellaneous Resources

Hanging Baskets, Window Boxes, and Other Container Gardens: A Guide to Creative Small-Scale Gardening, by David Joyce. Grades 9 and up. Published by Simon & Schuster, 200 Old Tappan Rd., Old Tappan, NJ 07675 (800) 223-2348.

Building Healthy Gardens: A Safe and Natural Approach, by Catharine Osgood Foster. Grades 9 and up. Published by Garden Way Publishing, Storey Communications, Schoolhouse Rd., Pownal, VT 05261. (800) 827-8673.

What About Ladybugs?, by Celia Godkin. Grades PreK-3. Published by Sierra Club Books. Distributed by Random House, 400 Hahn Rd., Westminster, MD 21157. (800) 733-3000.

Wonderful Worms, by Linda Glaser. Grades Pre-K-2. Published by Kingfisher Books, 95 Madison Ave., Suite 1205, New York, NY 10016. (800) 497-1657.

Encyclopedia of Country Living, by Carla Emery. Available from Farm Country General Store, Rte. 1, Box 63, Metamora, IL 61548. (800) 551-3276.

Opportunities in Horticulture Careers, by Jan Goldberg. Grades 9 and up. Published by VGM Career Horizons, a division of NTC Publishing Group, 4255 West Touhy Ave., Lincolnwood, IL 60646.

Reading Resources

The Secret Garden, by Frances Hodgson Burnett. Grades 4 and up. Published by HarperCollins Children's Books, 1000 Keystone Industrial Park, Scranton, PA 18512 (800) 242-7737.

The Secret Garden Study Guide, Grades 6-8. Published by Progeny Press, 1224 Round Hill Rd., Bryn Mawr, PA 19010. (610) 525-5446. Available from Shekinah Curriculum Cellar, P.O. Box 2154, Costa Mesa, CA 92628. (714) 751-7767.

Ox Cart Man, by Donald Hall. Grades PreK-3. Published by Puffin Books, Division of Penguin Books, P.O. Box 120, Bergenfield, NJ 07621. (800) 526-0275.

The Ox Cart Man Study Guide, Grades 1-3. Published by Progeny Press, 1224 Round Hill Rd., Bryn Mawr, PA 19010. (610) 525-5446. Available from Shekinah Curriculum Cellar, P.O. Box 2154, Costa Mesa, CA 92628. (714) 751-7767.

Rosy's Garden: A Child's Keepsake of Flowers, by Satomi Ichikawa and Elizabeth Laird. Published by Putnam Berkeley Group, 390 Murray Hill Parkway, East Rutherford, NJ 07073. (800) 631-8571.

The Rustling Grass, by Joanne DeJonge. Grades 4-8. Published by Eerdmans, 255 Jefferson Ave. SE, Grand Rapids, MI 49503. (800) 253-7521.

Raccoons & Ripe Corn, by Jim Arnosky. Grades PreK-3. Published by Lothrop, Division of William Morrow, P.O. Box 1219, West Caldwell, NJ 07007. (800) 237-0657. Available from: God's Riches, P.O. Box 560217, Miami, FL 33256-0217. (305) 667-3130.

A Garden's Blessing: Refreshment for the Soul, by Lois T. Chaplin. Published by Augsburg Fortress, 426 South Fifth, Box 1209, Minneapolis, MN 55440. (800) 848-2738.

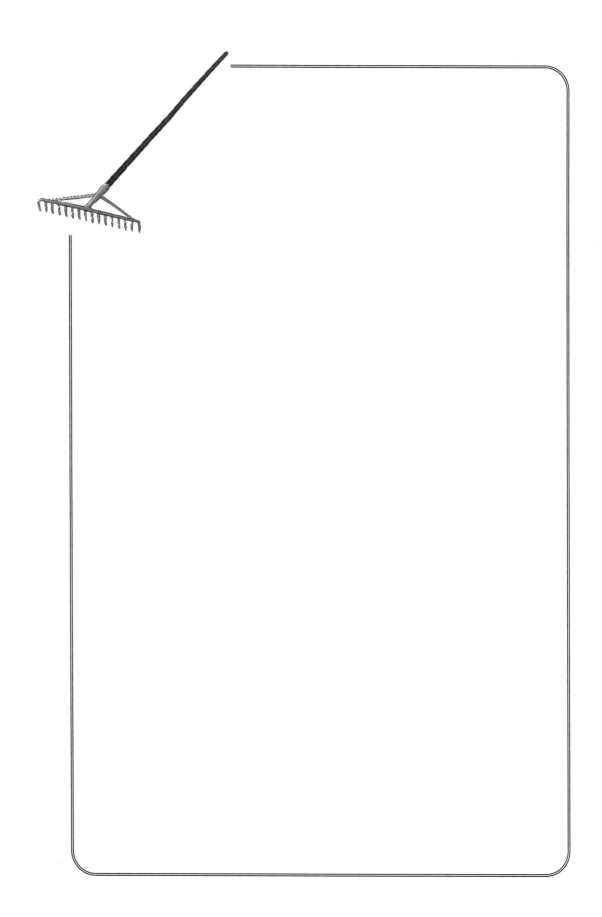

Strawberry Girl, by Lois Lenski. Grades K-6. Published by Bantam, Doubleday, Dell Publishing, 1540 Broadway, New York, NY 10036. (800) 223-6834.

The Bee Tree, by Patricia Polacco. Grades Pre-K to 3. Published by Philomel Books, 200 Madison Ave., New York, NY 10016.

Internet Resources

Here are some interesting sites on the Internet that you might want to visit while studying this unit. Please keep in mind that these pages, like all web pages, change from time to time. I recommend that you visit each site first, before the children do, to view the content and make sure that it meets your expectations. Also, use the **Subject Key Words** as search topics on Internet search engines, to find the latest additions that might pertain to this topic. (For help getting online, I highly recommend Homeschool Guide to the Online World — ISBN 1-888306-16-5.)

Burpee Seed Web Page:
http://garden.burpee.com

The Garden Gate on Prairienet:
http://www.prairienet.org/ag/garden/homepage.htm

The Garden Gate: Down the Garden Path:
http://www.prairienet.org/ag/garden/downpath.htm

The Garden Gate: Gardening Software:
http://www.prairienet.org/ag/garden/ereview.htm

GardenNet Guide to Gardens of the USA:
http://www.olympus.net/gardens/guide1.htm

Missouri Botanical GARDEN
http://www.mobot.org

Wildflowers:
http://rampages.onramp.net/~garylipe/

Wildflower Catalogs:
http://rampages.onramp.net/~garylipe/catalog.htm

The Gourmet Gardener:
http://metroux.metrobbs.com/tgg/catalog.htm

The Royal Botanic GARDENS, KEW (UK)
http://www.rbgkew.org.uk/index.html
American Association of Botanical Gardens & Arboreta
http://cissus.mobot.org/AABGA/aabga1.html

North American Rock GARDEN Society
http://www.mobot.org/NARGS/

GARDEN Holidays in Britain & Europe
http://www.u-net.com/tka/sisley/

GardenNet's Gardens On-line:
http://www.olympus.net/gardens/gardonln.htm

Amanda Bennett's Unit Study Web Page:
http://www.gocin.com/unit_study/

Working Outline

(This is the same outline as the one in the front of the unit study guide. However, spaces have been added between sections to provide room for writing, notes and diagrams used during the unit.)

I.   Introduction to gardens

    A.   Definition of a garden

    B.   Gardens and their role in history

        1.   Garden of Eden

        2.   Garden of Gethsemane

        3.   Gardens throughout the Bible

        4.   Gardens in later civilizations

    C.   Gardens around the world

    D.   Uses of garden

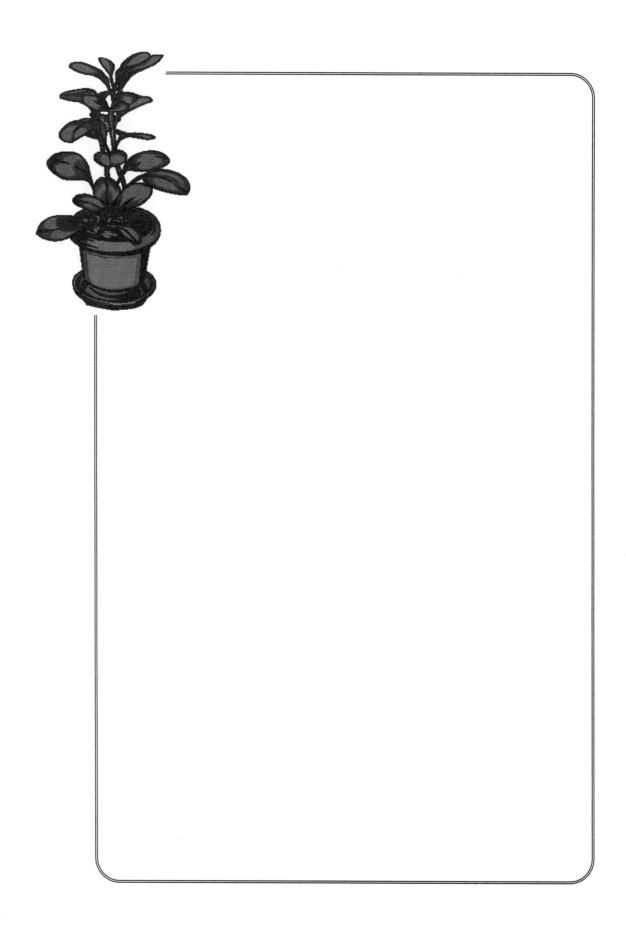

1. Provide food, herbs and flowers

2. Provide a source of pleasure and relaxation

3. Provide a place of beauty and relaxation to enjoy many kinds of plants and animals

E. Elements of a garden—appealing to the senses

1. Sight—visually appealing through the beauty of the plants as well, as the garden layout and other elements

2. Smell—the various scents of the plants and their fruit and flowers, as well as the smells of the tilled soil

3. Taste—enjoying the produce fresh from the garden

4. Sound—hearing the noises of the animal inhabitants (croaking toads, buzzing bees), as well as the sound of water running through a fountain or tinkling wind chimes

5. Touch—feeling the various textures of the many plants and their components

II.   Types of gardens

   A.   Rose garden

   B.   Flower garden

   C.   Vegetable garden

   D.   Victory garden

   E.   Kitchen garden

   F.   Oriental garden

   G.   Rock garden

   H.   Formal garden

   I.   Herb garden

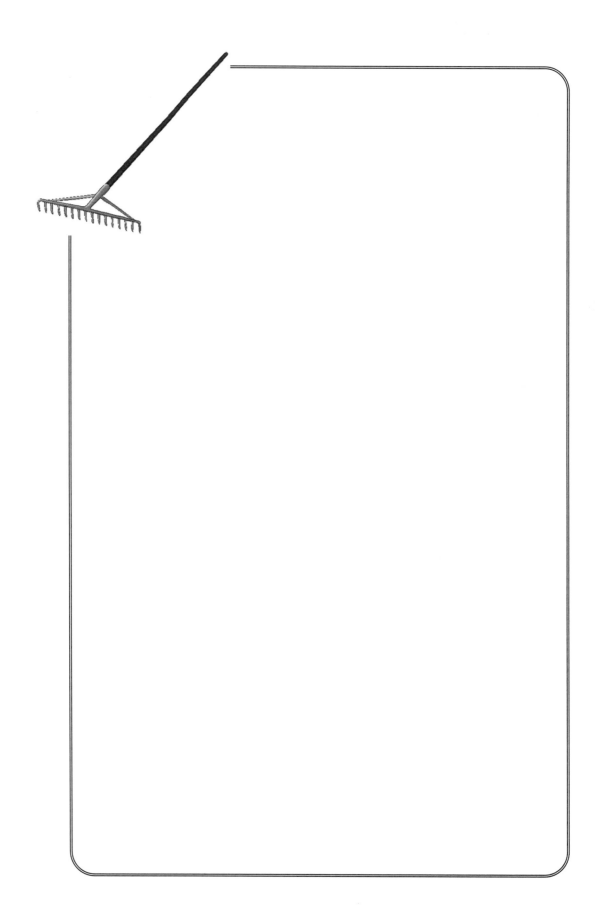

J.   Botanical garden

K.   Container garden

L.   Experimental garden

III.   History of gardens

A.   Beginning of time—Garden of Eden

B.   Spread of domestic crop plants throughout history

   1.   Early trade routes developed for trade of spices and herbs

   2.   Monks in medieval times developed herb gardens and studied herbal medicine

   3.   New World exploration

      a.   Early colonists learned about corn and crops for North America from the Indians

      b.   Explorers returned to Europe with many different types of plants and seeds from the new world

C. Gardens throughout time have usually been tended primarily by women—men were usually responsible for the tilling and soil preparation, and then the women took over, planting, weeding and maintaining the garden for the family.

D. Gardens had value for growing medicines for the family—herbs were believed to be the basis of their health and were added to the evening meal, usually soup with plenty of herbs which helped to prevent various ailments

E. Famous American gardens

    1.   Monticello—Thomas Jefferson

    2.   Mount Vernon—George Washington

    3.   The Hermitage—Andrew Jackson

    4.   White House Gardens

    5.   Winterthur in Delaware

6. National Arboretum in Washington, D.C.

   a. Early American Garden

   b. American Indian Garden

IV. Basic plant science

A. Plants form the base of the food chain, taking in inorganic elements and using them to produce organic compounds in their tissues

B. Some interesting fields of plant science that apply to gardens

   1. Botany

   2. Horticulture

   3. Agriculture

C. Uses of plants

   1. Provide food

      a. Vegetables

b.   Fruit

c.   Herbs and spices

2.   Provide medicines (quinine, digitalis)

3.   Provide elements for our shelter (wood)

4.   Provide energy resources (wood, fossil fuel)

5.   Provide clothing elements (cotton, flax)

D.   Plant science and structure (botany)

1.   Plant classification (taxonomy)

a.   Flowering division

b.   Nonflowering division

2. Differences in plants and animals

    a. Cell structure (this is a good time to introduce the use of a microscope, if possible)

    b. Food requirements

    c. Food for plant growth is manufactured by a process called photosynthesis, utilizing chlorophyll

3. Basic plant structure

    a. Roots

        (1) Fibrous root system

        (2) Tap root system

    b. Stem

        (1) Types of stem

            (a) Woody

            (b) Herbaceous

(2)   Circulatory system

    (a)   Xylem tissue

    (b)   Phloem tissue

c.   Leaf

  (1)   Leaf blade

    (a)   Leaf base

    (b)   Midrib

    (c)   Margin

    (d)   Vein

  (2)   Petiole

  (3)   Apex

d.   Flower

  (1)   Petal

  (2)   Sepal

  (3)   Stamen

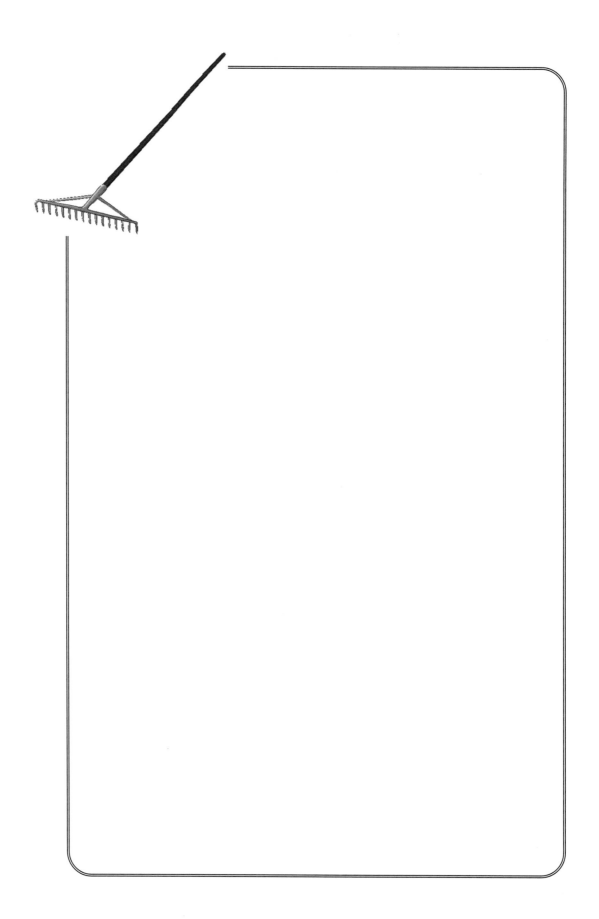

            (4)   Pollen

            (5)   Stigma

            (6)   Pistil

            (7)   Ovule

    e.   Seed

            (1)   Seed coat

            (2)   Embryo

            (3)   Cotyledon

            (4)   Endosperm

E.   Plant requirements

    1.   Water

    2.   Air

3. Nutrients

4. Sunshine

F. Geography and plants

    1. Different areas of the world can support various plants

    2. Zones have been named for these land areas of the world

        a. Desert

        b. Forest

        c. Grassland

        d. Mountain

        e. Rainforest

f.   Tropic

g.   Tundra

3.   The U.S. Department of Agriculture has developed hardiness zones for the United States, based on minimum temperatures for each zone (usually displayed in American seed catalogs)

V.   Your own garden

A.   Locate the garden, and consider these important factors

1.   Daily hours of sunlight

2.   Good drainage

3.   Soil quality

4.   Water availability

5.   Wind protection

B.   Plan the garden

    1.   Determine the size of space available for the garden

    2.   Consider crops that grow well in your area

        a.   Climate

        b.   Season

        c.   Soil quality

    3.   Design different gardens for different seasons

        a.   Cool weather crops

        b.   Warm weather crops

    4.   Popular home garden plants

        a.   Vegetables

           (1)   Tomatoes

           (2)   Green beans

(3)   Peas

(4)   Cucumbers

(5)   Radishes

(6)   Carrots

(7)   Squash

(8)   Pumpkins

(9)   Watermelon

(10) Eggplant

(11) Onions

(12) Potatoes

(13) Strawberries

(14) Lettuce

(15) Peppers

b. Herbs

   (1) Mint

   (2) Oregano

   (3) Sweet basil

   (4) Chives

   (5) Parsley

   (6) Dill

   (7) Rosemary

c. Flowers

   (1) Marigolds

   (2) Zinnias

   (3) Sunflowers

   (4) Pansies

   (5) Petunias

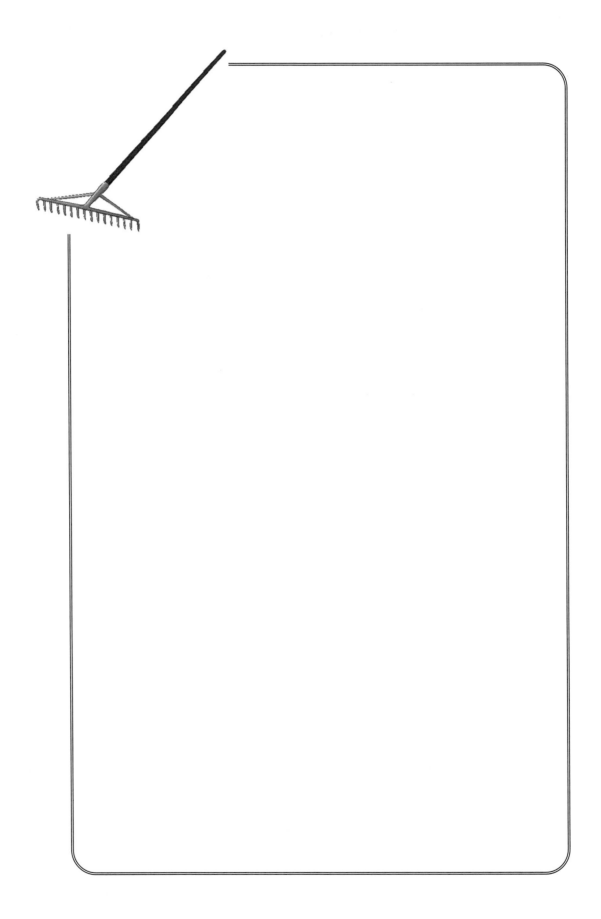

(6)   Impatiens

(7)   Snapdragons

(8)   Sweet peas

C.   Prepare the soil

    1.   Till and remove rocks, roots and other debris

    2.   Test a sample of the soil to determine the chemistry of your soil at the garden site

        a.   Testing is usually available through the County Extension service

        b.   Use soil test results, and add ingredients to the soil to improve the fertility and adjust the chemistry, if needed

    3.   Add nutrients to the soil to enrich the soils organic matter

        a.   Compost

        b.   Fertilizer

D. Plant the garden

    1. Seeds

    2. Seedlings

        a. Purchase at local nurseries

        b. Purchase through plant and seed catalogs

        c. Start them in your home from seed

    3. Bulbs

E. Maintain the garden

    1. Feeding

        a. Fertilizing

        b. Composting

    2. Watering

        a. Rain

b. Irrigation

3. Insects in the garden

    a. Helpful insects

        (1) Earthworms

        (2) Bees

        (3) Ladybugs

        (4) Praying mantises

    b. Harmful insects

        (1) Beetles

        (2) Caterpillars

        (3) Aphids

    c. Controlling harmful insects

        (1) Natural methods

        (2) Chemical methods

d.   Other considerations

    (1)   Birds

    (2)   Small animals (rabbits, raccoons)

4.   Weeding/mulching

a.   Weeding helps make certain that nutrients and water are used by crops, instead of weeds

b.   Mulching helps to minimize weed growth and conserve soil moisture and many different materials can be used

    (1)   Shredded wood bark

    (2)   Newspaper

    (3)   Plastic sheets

    (4)   Leaves

    (5)   Compost

F.   Harvest the garden's produce

1.   Pick crops when ripe

2.   Enjoy the produce fresh

3.   Preserve the produce

   a.   Canning

   b.   Freezing

   c.   Drying

VI.   Famous scientists, gardeners and planters

A.   Gregor Mendel

B.   George Washington Carver

C.   Thomas Jefferson

D.   Monet (Claude Monet)

E.   John Chapman (Johnny Appleseed)

VII. Art and gardens

A. Famous artists that painted gardens and natural elements

    1. Monet (Claude Monet)

        a. *The Artist's Garden at Giverny*

        b. *Women in the Garden*

        c. *The Artist's Garden at Vétheuil*

        d. *Water Lilies*

    2. Beatrix Potter

    3. Van Gogh

    4. Renoir

B. Still life paintings of garden produce

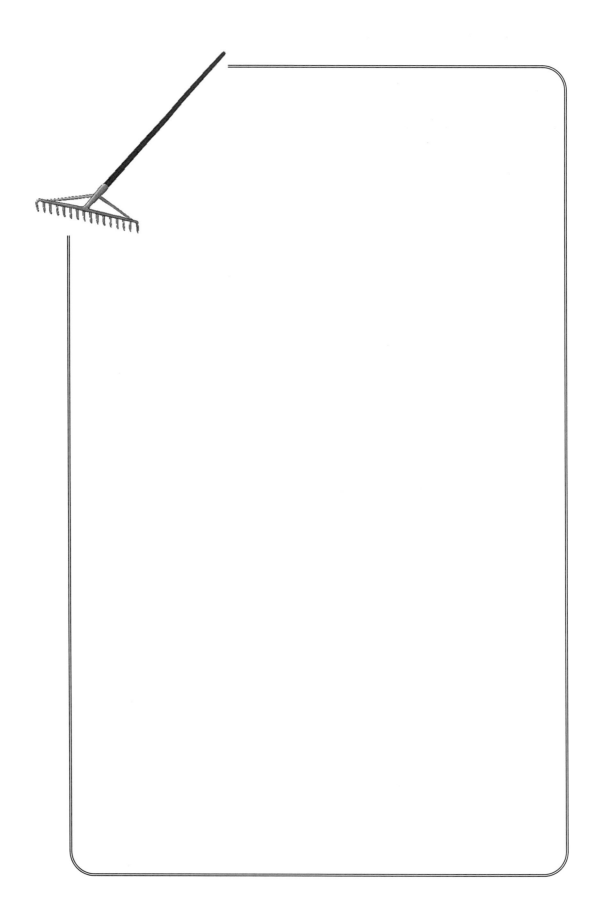

C.   Nature sketches in garden settings

VIII. Poetry and gardens

A.   *A Child's Garden of Verses,* by Robert Louis Stevenson

     1.   "The Flowers"

     2.   "The Gardener"

     3.   "Summer Sun"

     4.   "Farewell to the Farm"

B.   *The Door at the End of Our Garden,* by Frederick Weatherly

About The Author

Amanda Bennett, author and speaker, wife and mother of three, holds a degree in mechanical engineering. She has written this ever-growing series of unit studies for her own children, to capture their enthusiasm and nurture their gifts and talents. The concept of a thematic approach to learning is a simple one. Amanda will share this simplification through her books, allowing others to use these unit study guides to discover the amazing world that God has created for us all.

Science can be a very intimidating subject to teach, and Amanda has written this series to include science with other important areas of curriculum that apply naturally to each topic. The guides allow more time to be spent enjoying the unit study, instead of spending weeks of research time to prepare for each unit. She has shared the results of her research in the guides, including plenty of resources for areas of the study, spelling and vocabulary lists, fiction and nonfiction titles, possible careers within the topic, writing ideas, activity suggestions, addresses of manufacturers, teams, and other helpful resources.

The science-based series of guides currently includes the Unit Study Adventures titles:

Baseball	Oceans
Computers	Olympics
Elections	Pioneers
Electricity	Space
Flight	Trains
Gardens	
Homes	

The holiday-based series of guides currently includes the Unit Study Adventures titles:

Christmas
Thanksgiving

This planned 40-book series will soon include additional titles, which will be released periodically. We appreciate your interest. "Enjoy the Adventure."